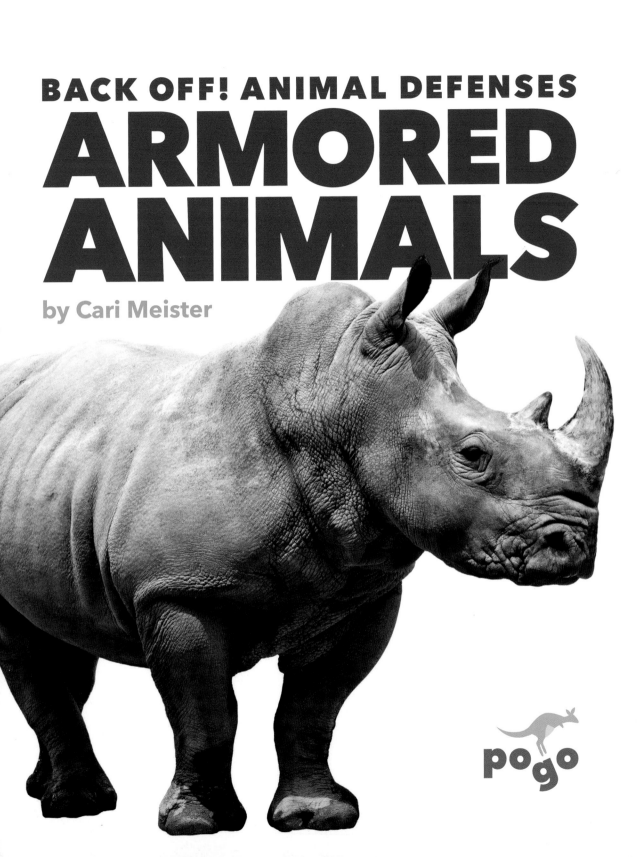

BACK OFF! ANIMAL DEFENSES
ARMORED ANIMALS

by Cari Meister

pogo

Ideas for Parents and Teachers

Pogo Books let children practice reading informational text while introducing them to nonfiction features such as headings, labels, sidebars, maps, and diagrams, as well as a table of contents, glossary, and index.

Carefully leveled text with a strong photo match offers early fluent readers the support they need to succeed.

Before Reading

- "Walk" through the book and point out the various nonfiction features. Ask the student what purpose each feature serves.
- Look at the glossary together. Read and discuss the words.

Read the Book

- Have the child read the book independently.
- Invite him or her to list questions that arise from reading.

After Reading

- Discuss the child's questions. Talk about how he or she might find answers to those questions.
- Prompt the child to think more. Ask: Have you seen any of the armored animals mentioned in the book? Can you think of any armored animals that aren't discussed?

Pogo Books are published by Jump!
5357 Penn Avenue South
Minneapolis, MN 55419
www.jumplibrary.com

Library of Congress Cataloging-in-Publication Data

Meister, Cari, author.
  Armored animals / by Cari Meister.
    pages cm. – (Back off! Animal defenses)
  Audience: Ages 7-10.
  Summary: "Carefully leveled text and vibrant photographs introduce readers to armored animals such as the crab, armadillo, pangolin, and all kinds of beetles, and explore how they use armor to defend themselves against predators. Includes activity, glossary, and index."–Provided by publisher.
  Includes bibliographical references and index.
  ISBN 978-1-62031-308-4 (hardcover: alk. paper)
  ISBN 978-1-62496-374-2 (ebook)
  1. Animal defenses–Juvenile literature.
  2. Armored animals–Juvenile literature. I. Title.
  QL759.M454 2016
  591.47'7–dc23

                                    2015033966

Series Editor: Jenny Fretland VanVoorst
Series Designer: Anna Peterson
Book Designer: Lindaanne Donohoe
Photo Researcher: Jenny Fretland VanVoorst

Photo Credits: Alamy, 4, 5, 8-9, 10, 12-13; Nature Picture Library, 11; Shutterstock, cover, 6-7, 14-15, 20-21; SuperStock, 17, 18-19; Thinkstock, 23.

Printed in the United States of America at Corporate Graphics in North Mankato, Minnesota.

TABLE OF CONTENTS

CHAPTER 1
Scales and Skin 4

CHAPTER 2
Bony Plates 10

CHAPTER 3
Exoskeletons 16

ACTIVITIES & TOOLS
Try This! 22
Glossary 23
Index 24
To Learn More 24

CHAPTER 1

SCALES AND SKIN

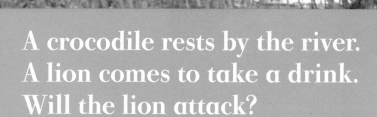

A crocodile rests by the river.
A lion comes to take a drink.
Will the lion attack?

No! The croc's skin is too thick and tough. The lion does not bother him.

How do you stay alive when you share a **habitat** with tigers? For one thing, you need to be big. An Indian rhinoceros weighs about 4,400 pounds (2,000 kilograms). That's as much as a big car!

Size is not the only reason tigers do not hunt rhinos. Rhinos have thick, armor-like skin. Even a tiger would have a hard time cutting through two to five centimeters of rhino skin!

A rhino's skin comes in handy when fighting other rhinos. It protects its body from stabbing horns.

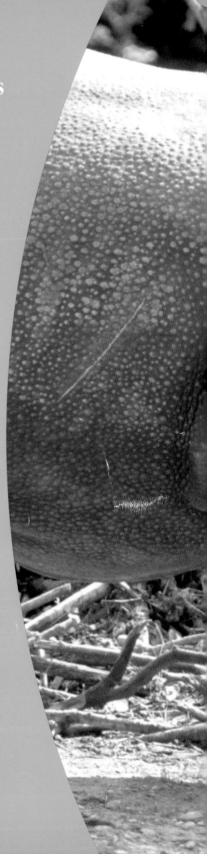

CHAPTER 2

BONY PLATES

A pangolin digs in the dirt with her long claws. What is she looking for? Dinner!

Bullseye! She finds a termite nest. But look! The termites **swarm** her. They bite. They bite and bite, but they cannot get through her horny scales. She keeps eating.

A lion is hunting nearby. He sees the pangolin. He pounces. She rolls in a ball. The lion swats, but the pangolin is protected by her scales. The lion bites, but the scales are too hard. He gives up. She is safe.

scutes

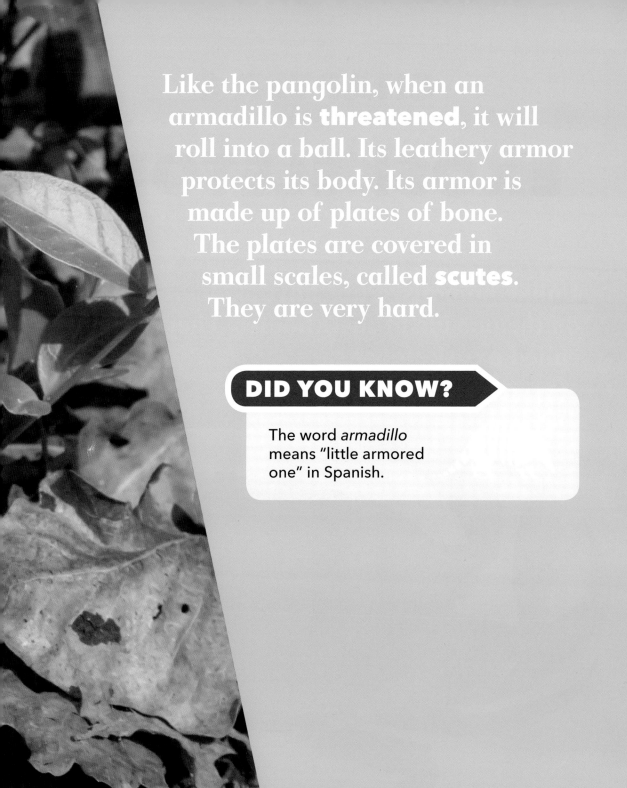

Like the pangolin, when an armadillo is **threatened**, it will roll into a ball. Its leathery armor protects its body. Its armor is made up of plates of bone. The plates are covered in small scales, called **scutes**. They are very hard.

DID YOU KNOW?

The word *armadillo* means "little armored one" in Spanish.

CHAPTER 3

EXOSKELETONS

Unlike humans, crabs have skeletons on the outside of their bodies. They are called **exoskeletons.**

Many animals do not eat crabs because of their hard shells.

But birds carry crabs into the air. Then, they drop them onto rocks. The shells break. Yum! Crab meat.

A crab walks by a **tide pool**. Look out! An octopus comes out of the tide pool and grabs the crab. He pulls the crab underwater. The crab tries to fight. Will its hard shell keep it safe? Not this time. The octopus has a sharp **beak**. It smashes the crab's shell.

A beetle has hard outer wings called **elytra**. They act like armor for its soft wings inside. They make it hard for birds to bite.

TAKE A LOOK

There are more kinds of beetles than any other kind of animal. There are more than 350,000 different beetles. In fact, one out of every four animals is a beetle.

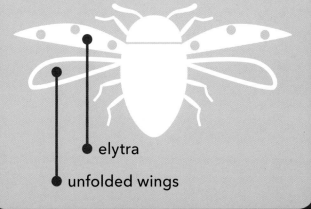

elytra

unfolded wings

ACTIVITIES & TOOLS

PROTECTIVE ARMOR

Explore the world of animal armor.

You will need:

- a thick piece of leather (or a leather jacket)
- a hard piece of plastic
- a variety of large shells
- a sweatshirt
- some other materials of your choice
- a friend

Steps:

❶ Gather the materials.

❷ Have one person be the predator and one person the prey.

❸ Put a piece of leather around the prey's arm.

❹ The predator will use his or her fingers as if they were teeth and grab a hold of the prey's arm. How much can the prey feel?

❺ Do the same thing with all of the different materials.

❻ Which type of material gave the best protection from the predator's "mouth"?

❼ What animals from the book do the different materials represent?

GLOSSARY

beak: A hard, sharp, pointed mouth part.

elytra: Hard outer wings.

exoskeleton: The hard outer covering that protects an animal's soft body.

habitat: The place an animal lives.

scutes: Hard, small, horny scales.

swarm: To attack in a large group.

threatened: In danger.

tide pool: Places near ocean rocks that fill with seawater.

INDEX

armadillo 15

armor 8, 15, 21

ball 12, 15

beetle 21

bone 15

crab 16, 17, 18

crocodile 4, 5

elytra 21

exoskeletons 16

habitat 7

horns 8

pangolin 10, 11, 12, 15

rhinoceros 7, 8

scales 11, 12, 15

scutes 15

shell 17, 18

skeletons 16

skin 5, 8

tide pool 18

wings 21

TO LEARN MORE

Learning more is as easy as 1, 2, 3.

1) Go to www.factsurfer.com

2) Enter "armoredanimals" into the search box.

3) Click the "Surf" button to see a list of websites.

With factsurfer, finding more information is just a click away.